I0462950

# FERRET

# COLORING BOOK

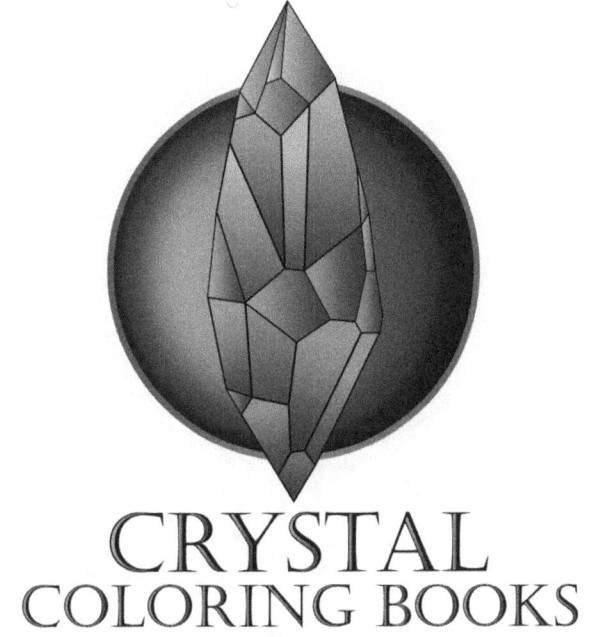

# CRYSTAL
## COLORING BOOKS

ISBN: 9781081156664

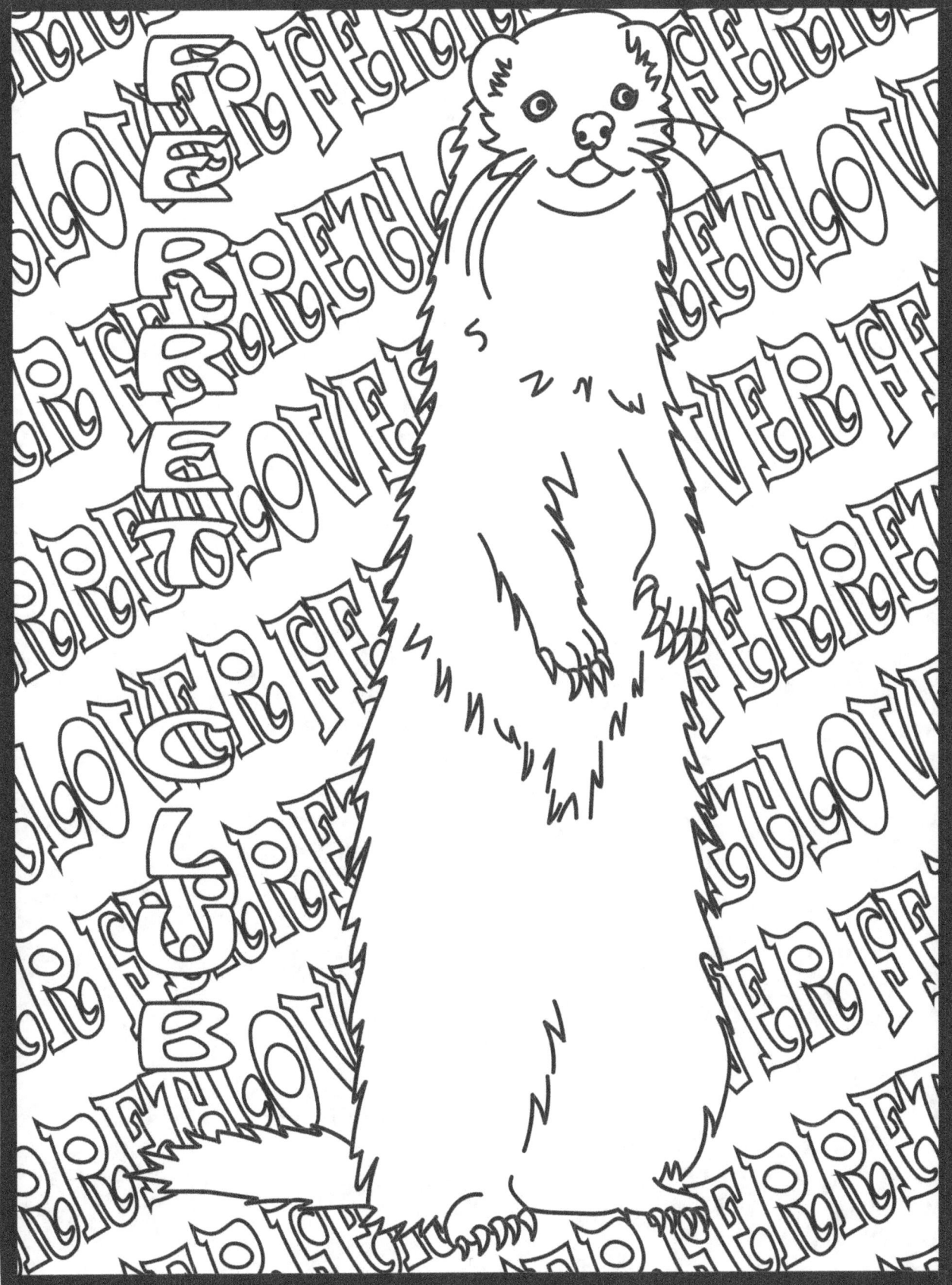

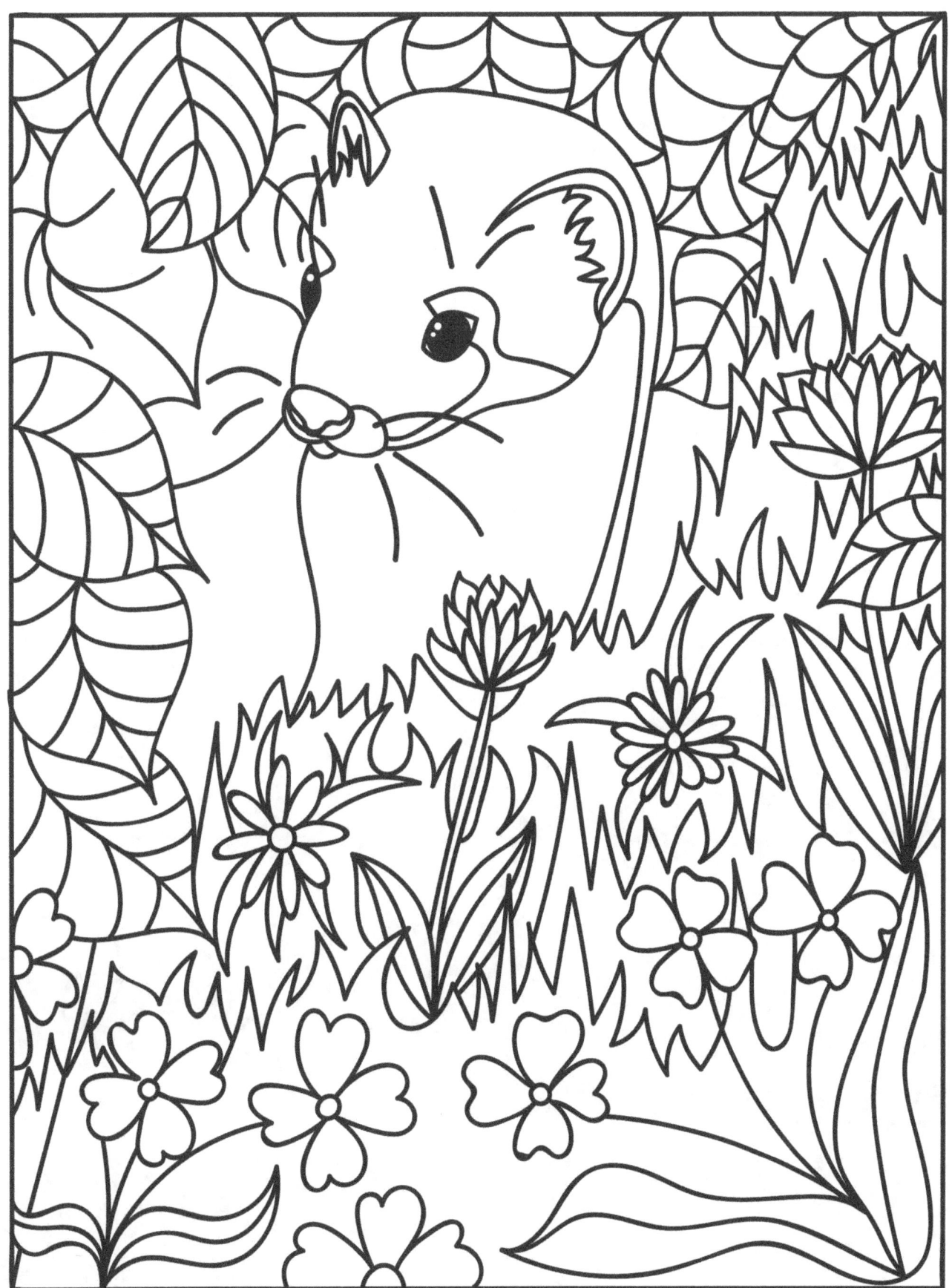

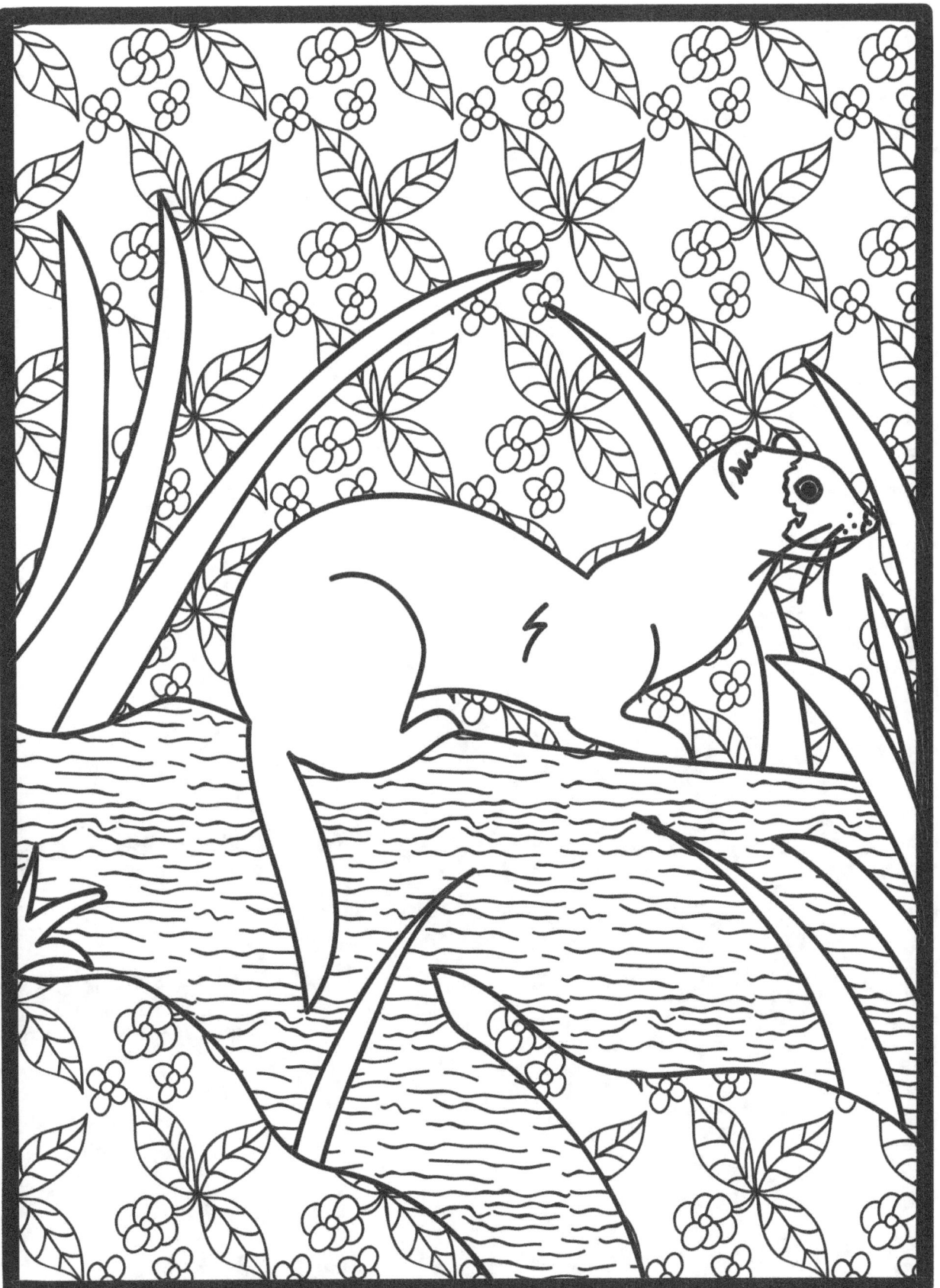

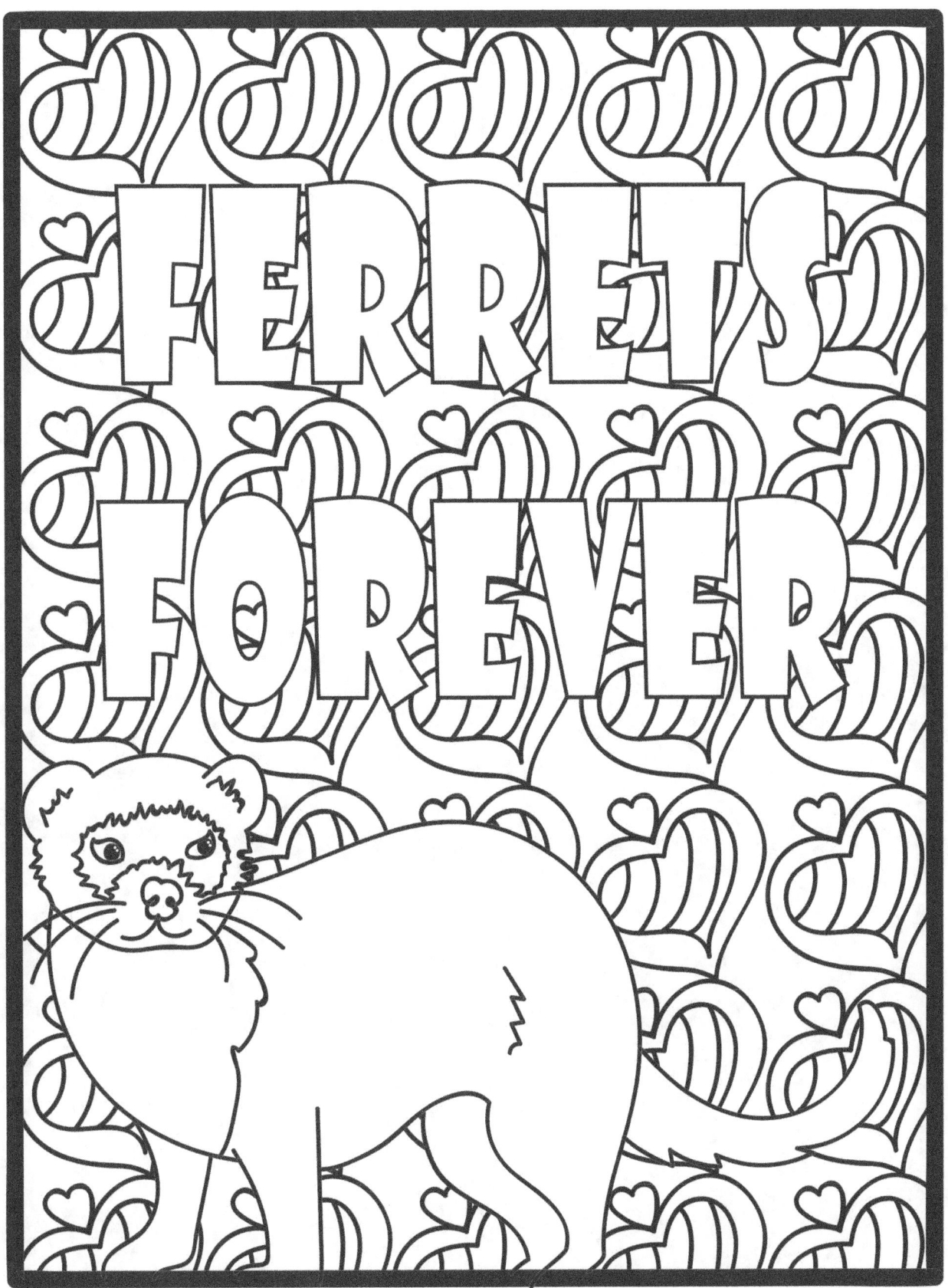

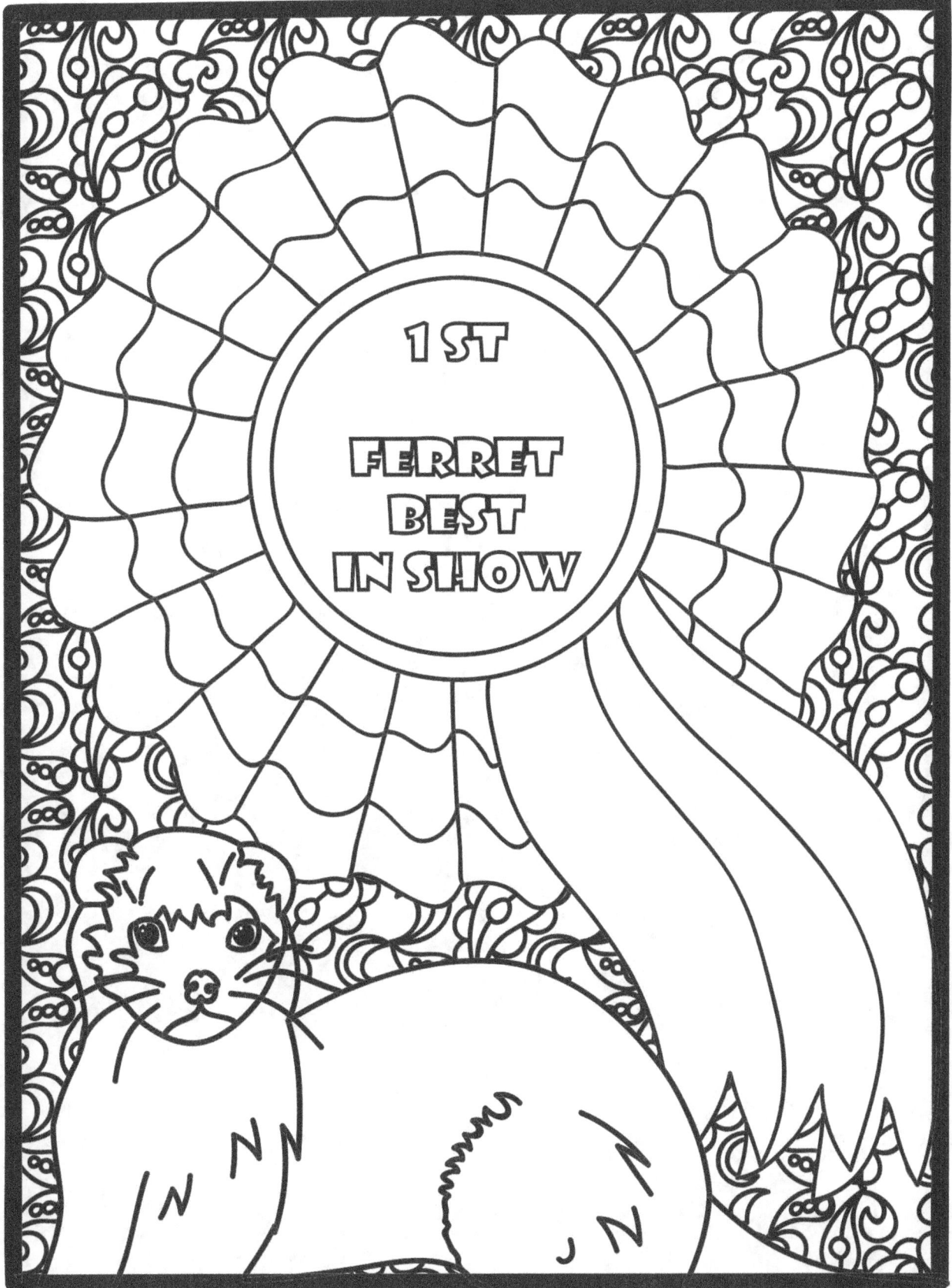

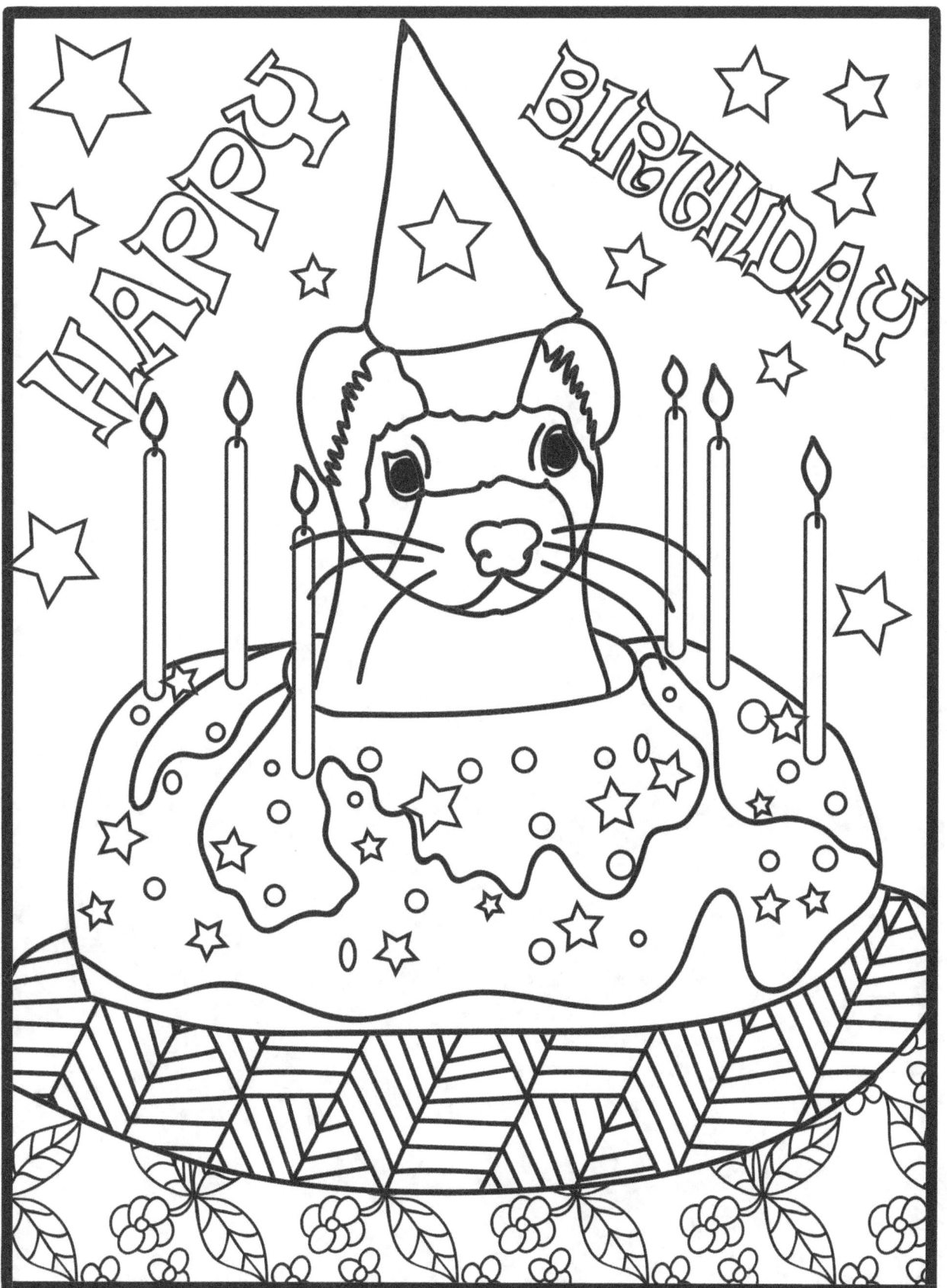

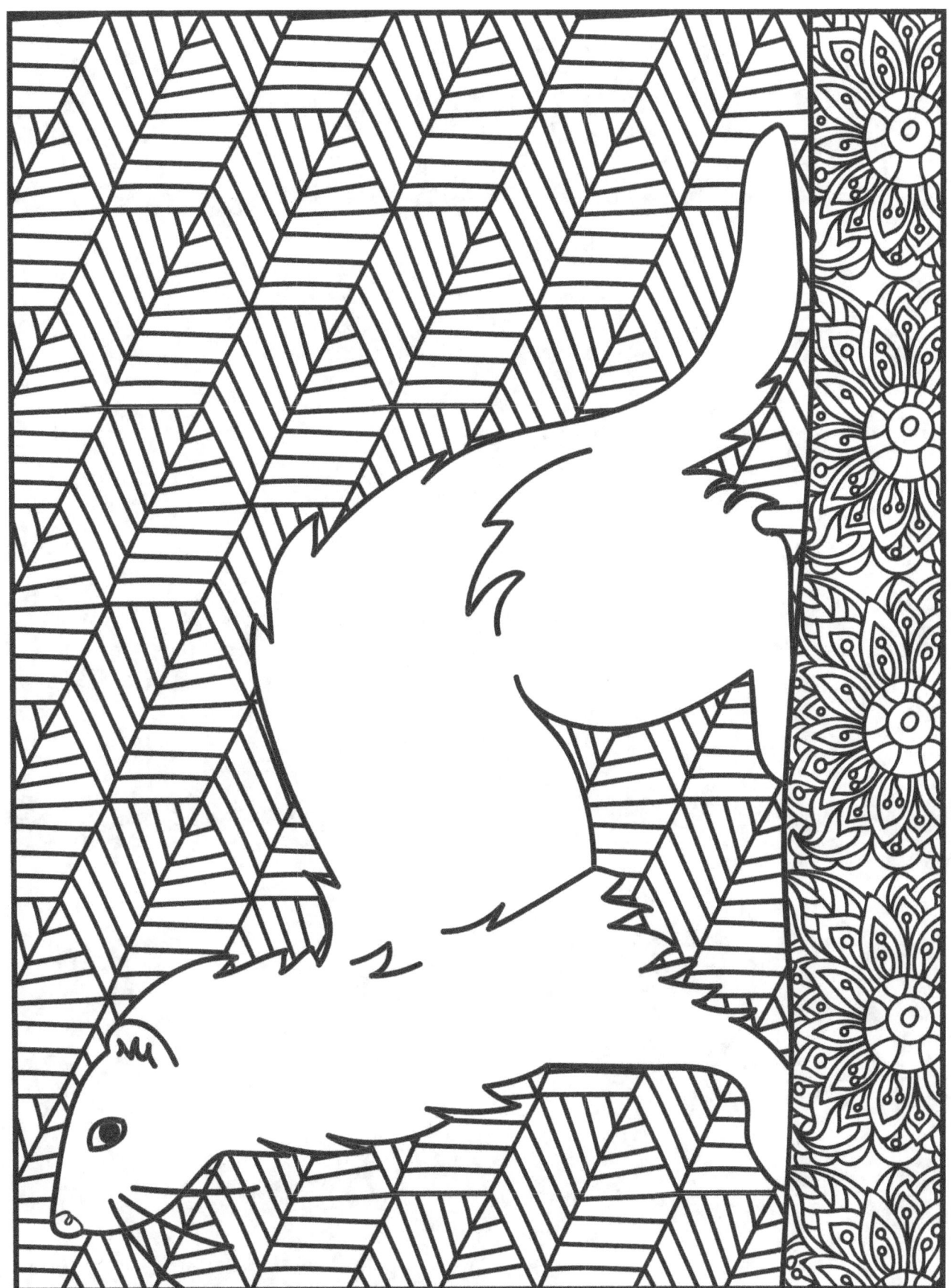

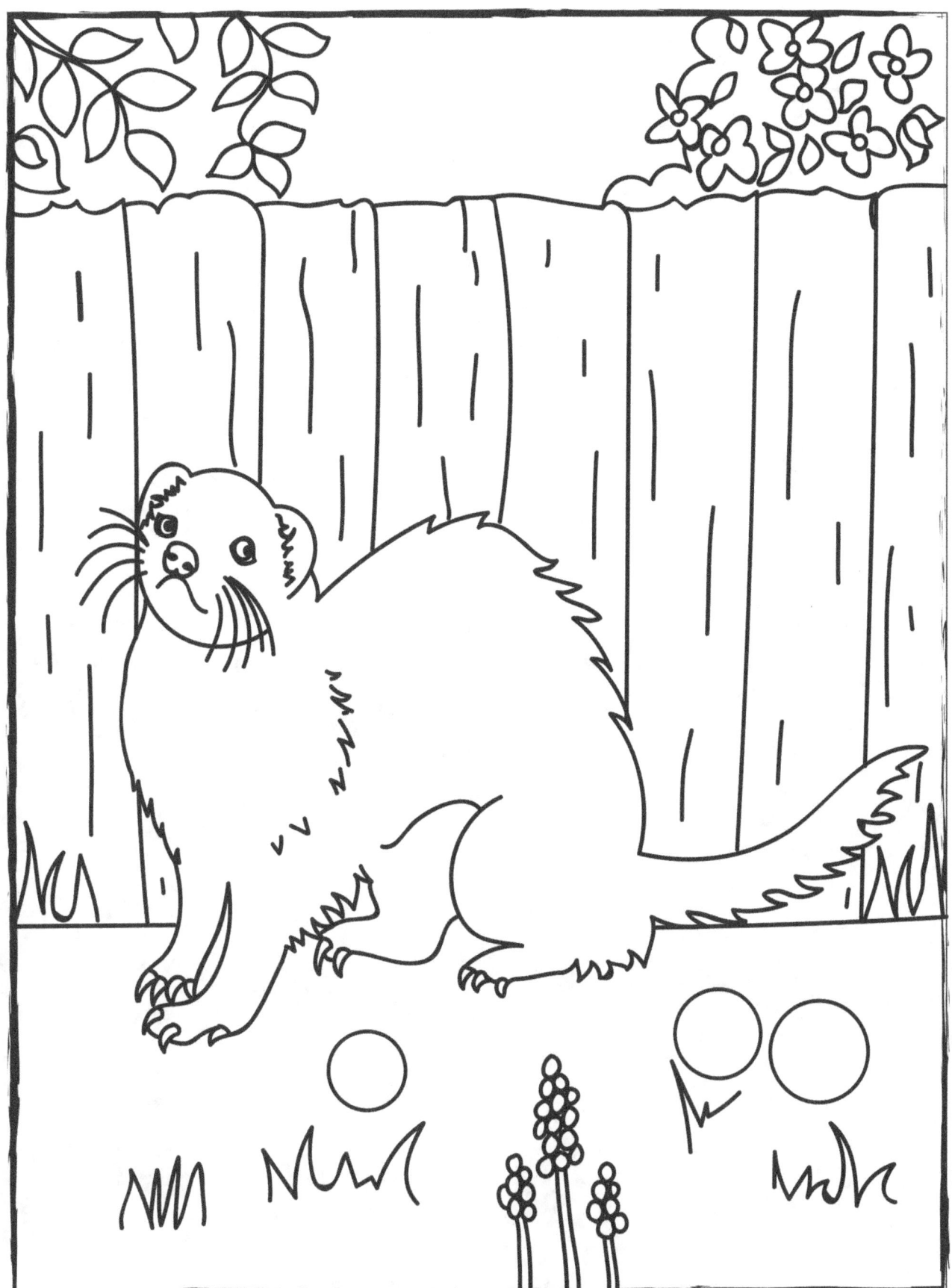

I LOVE MY FERRET

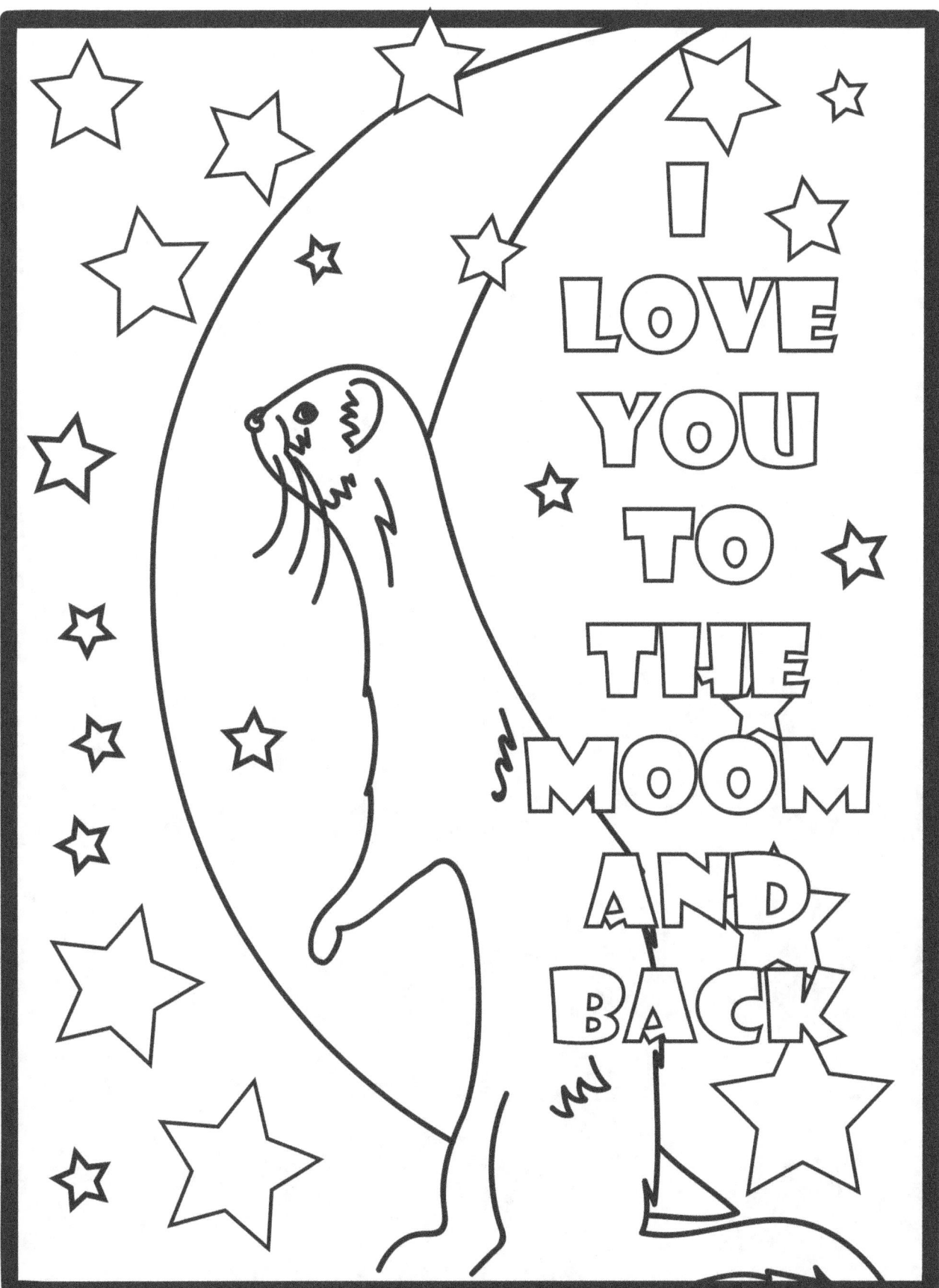

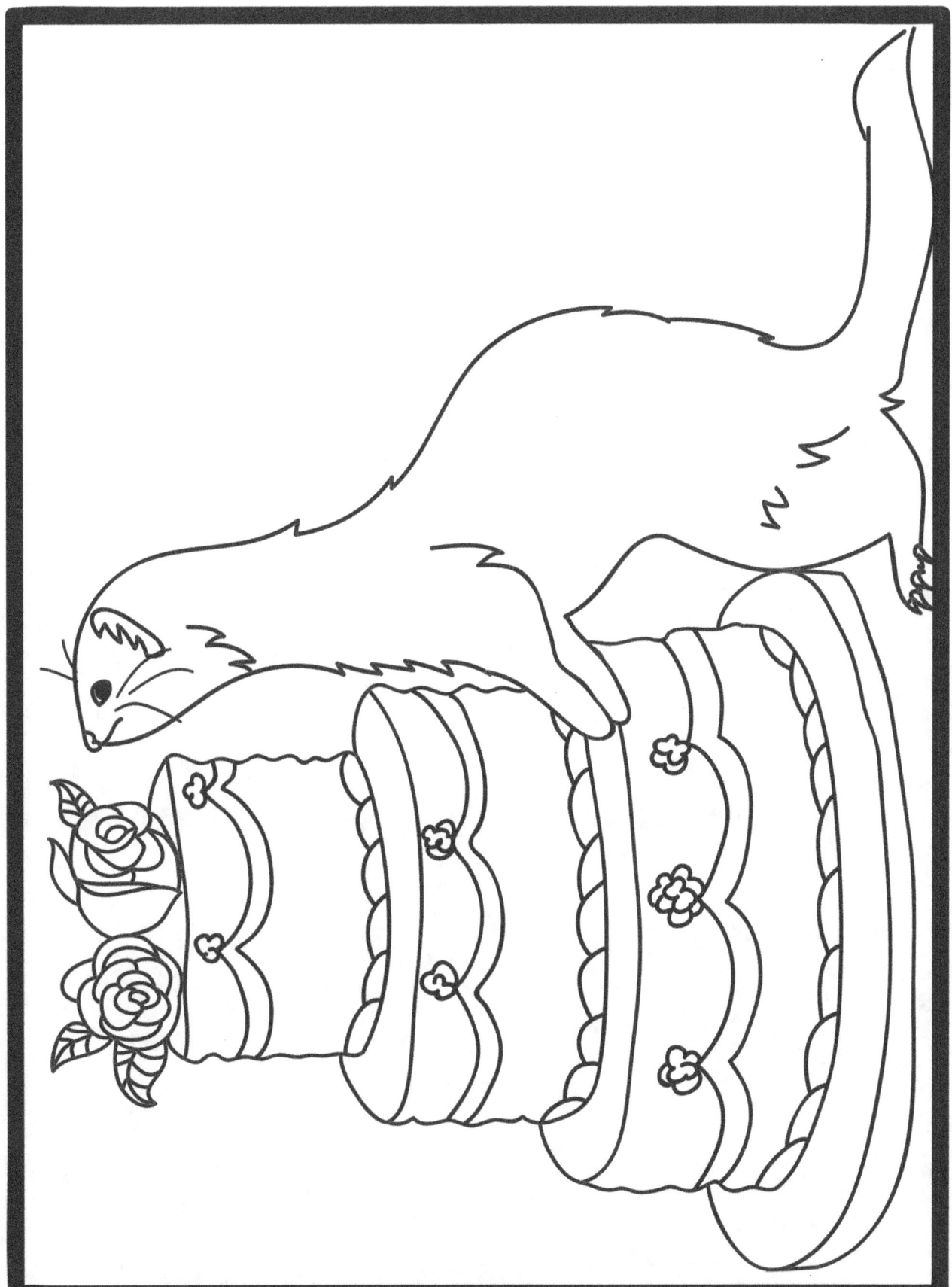

NUMBER 1

FERRET FAN

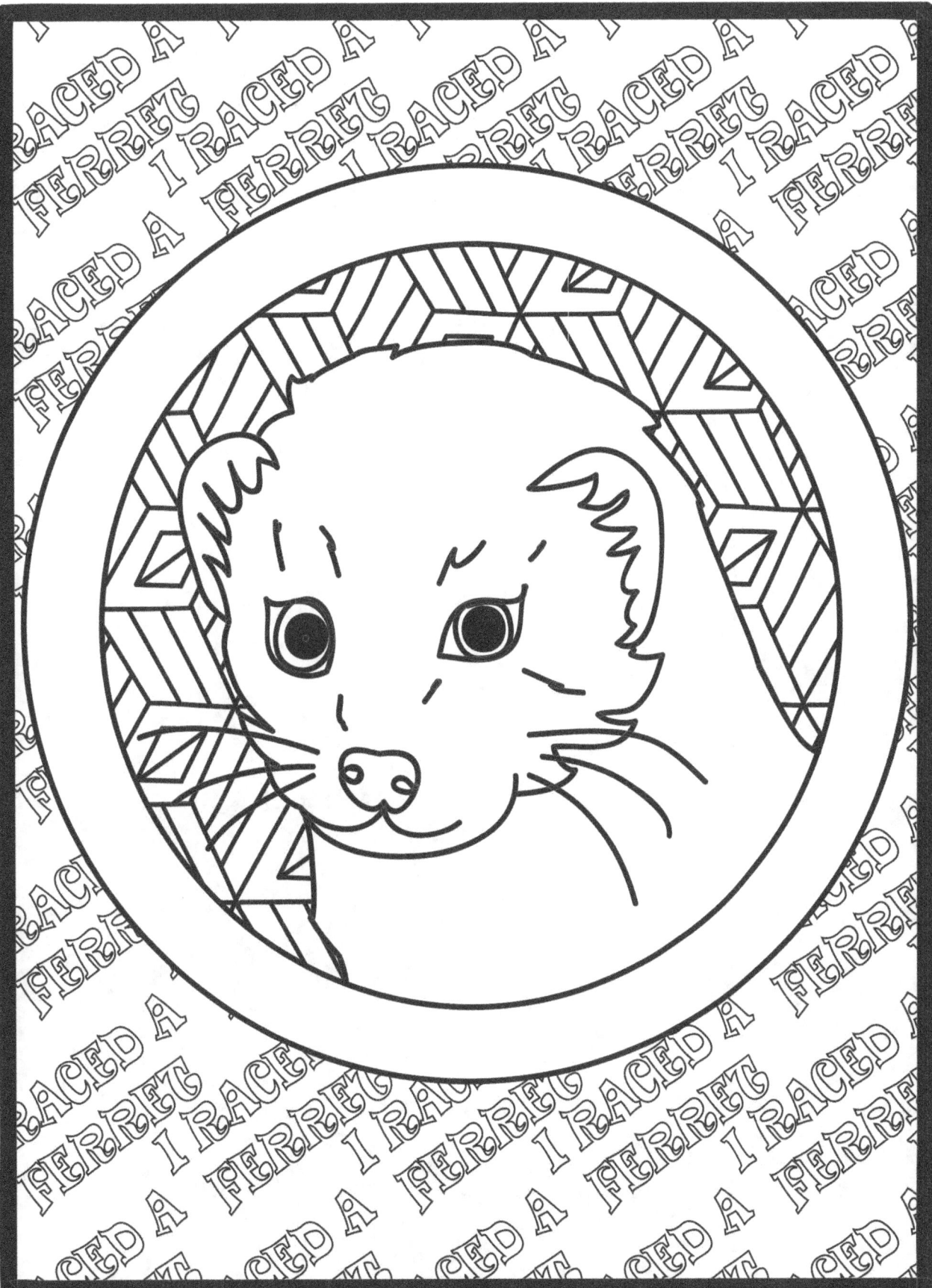

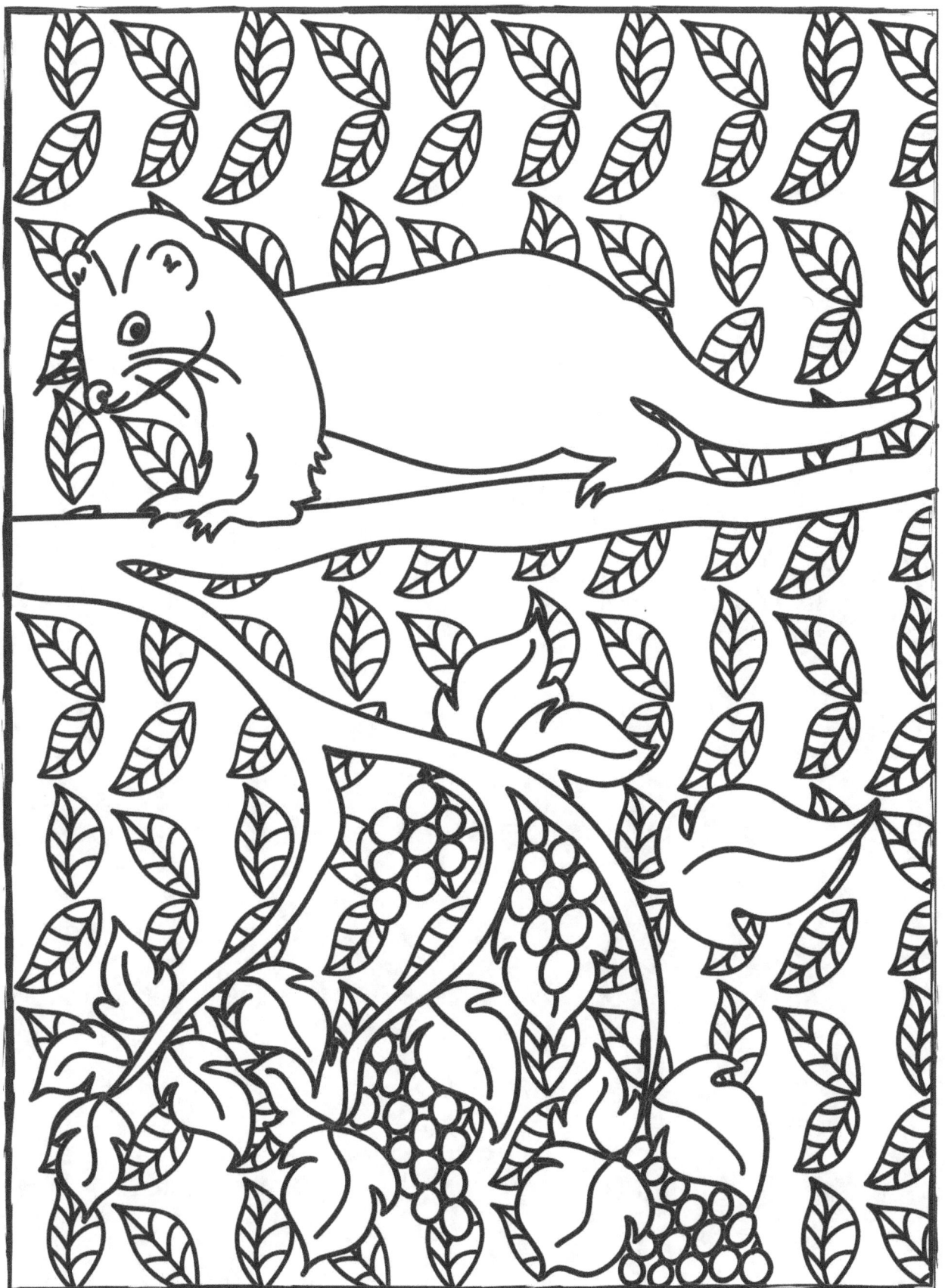

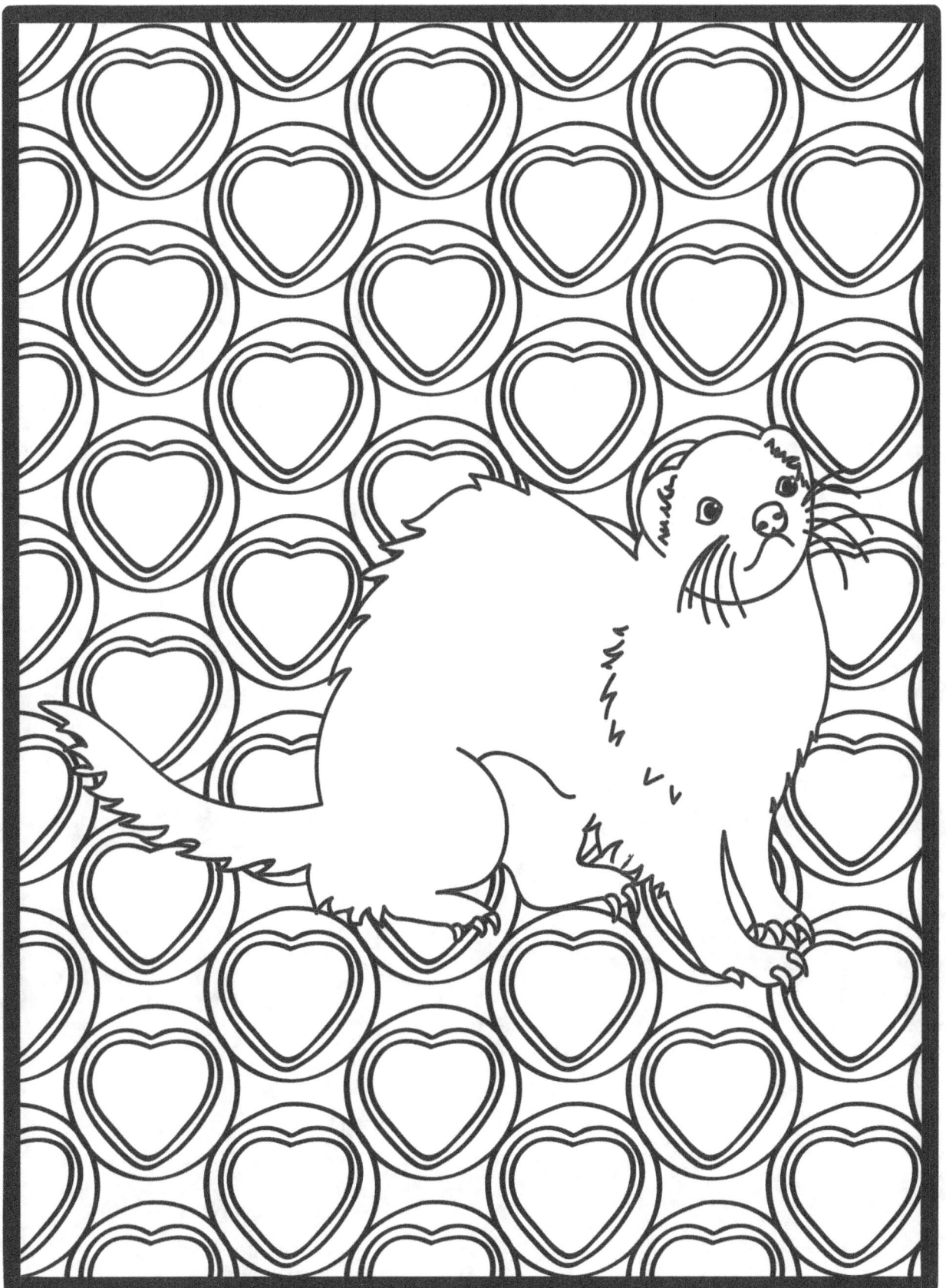

# #FERRET FAN

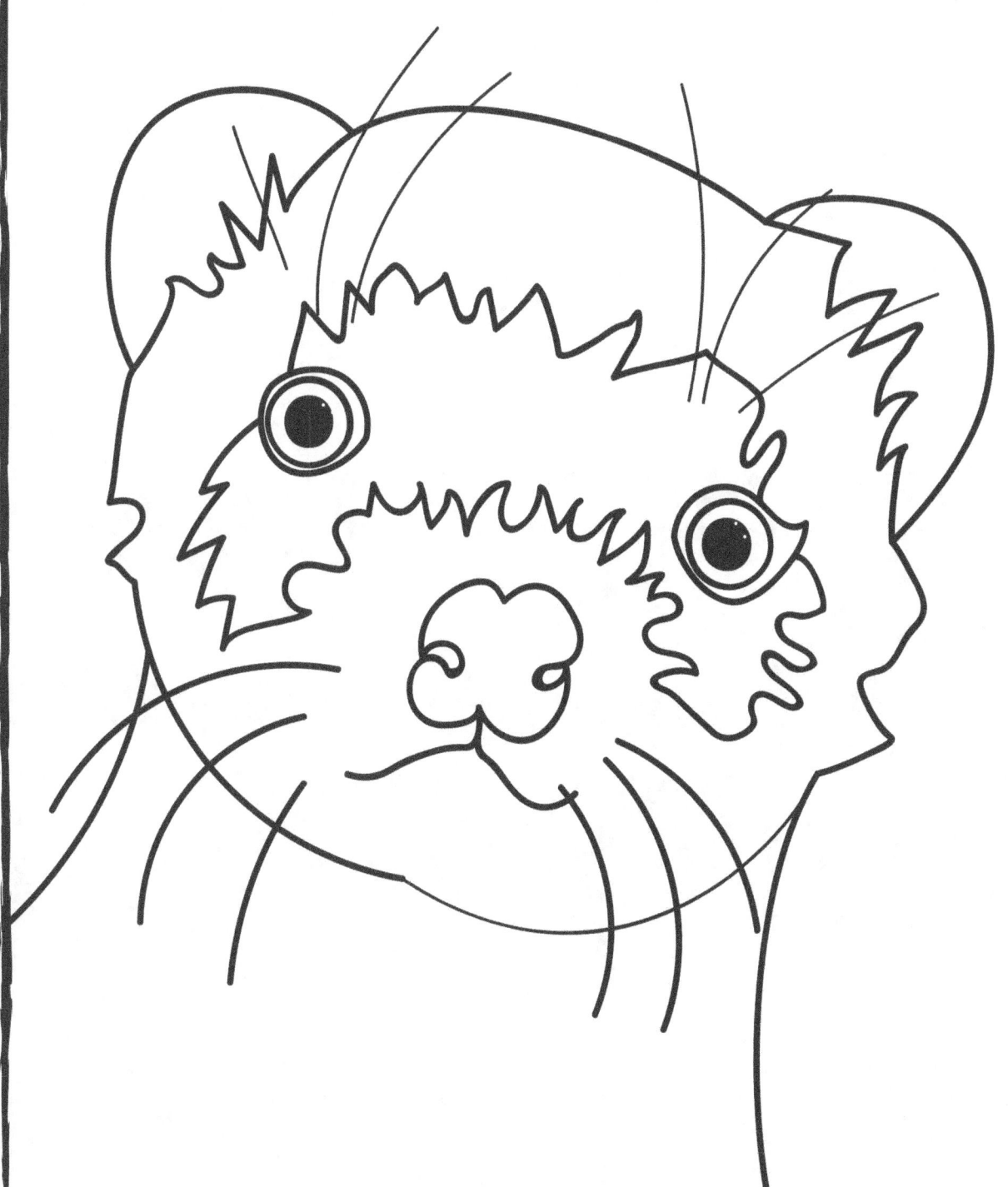

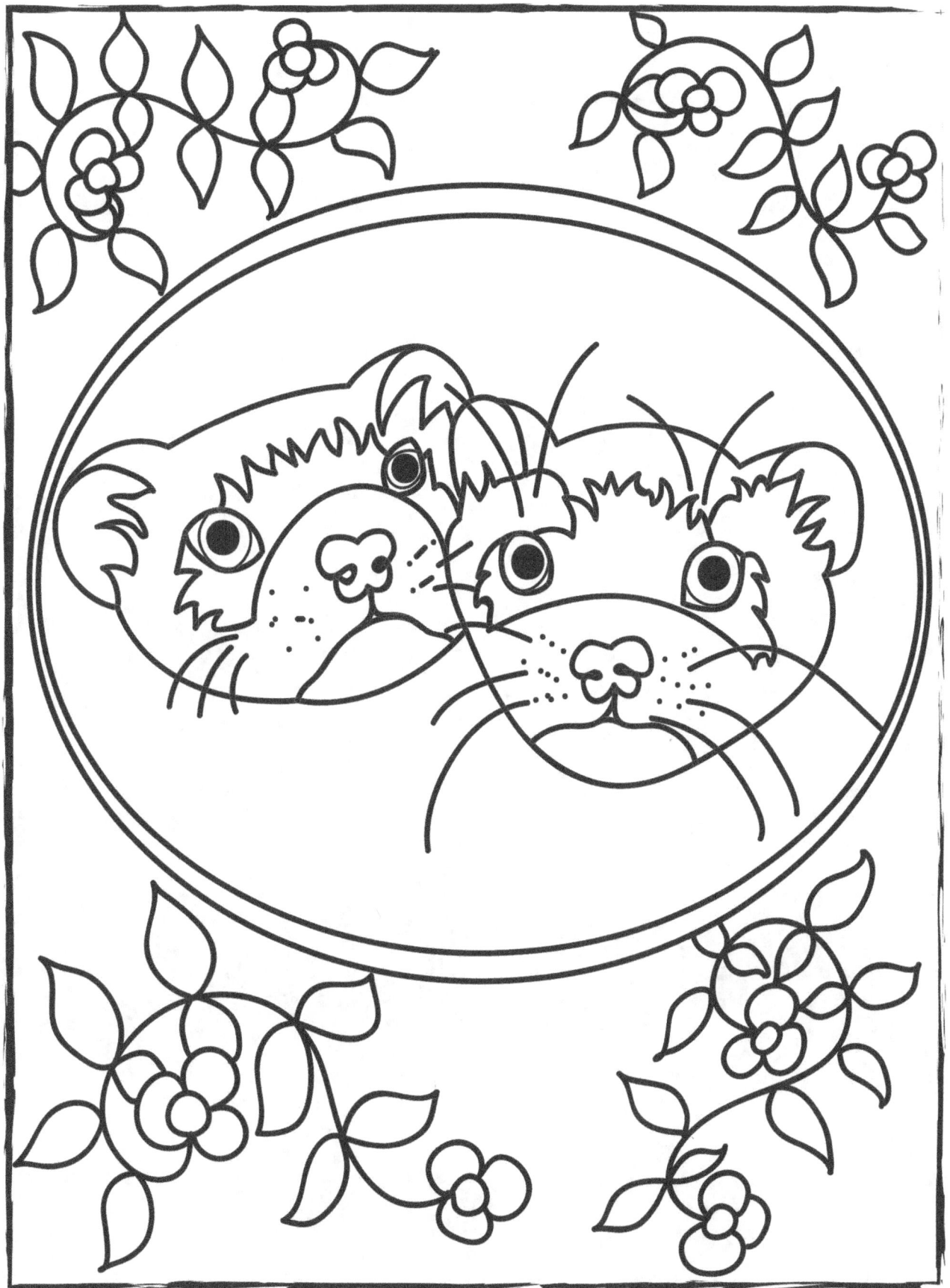

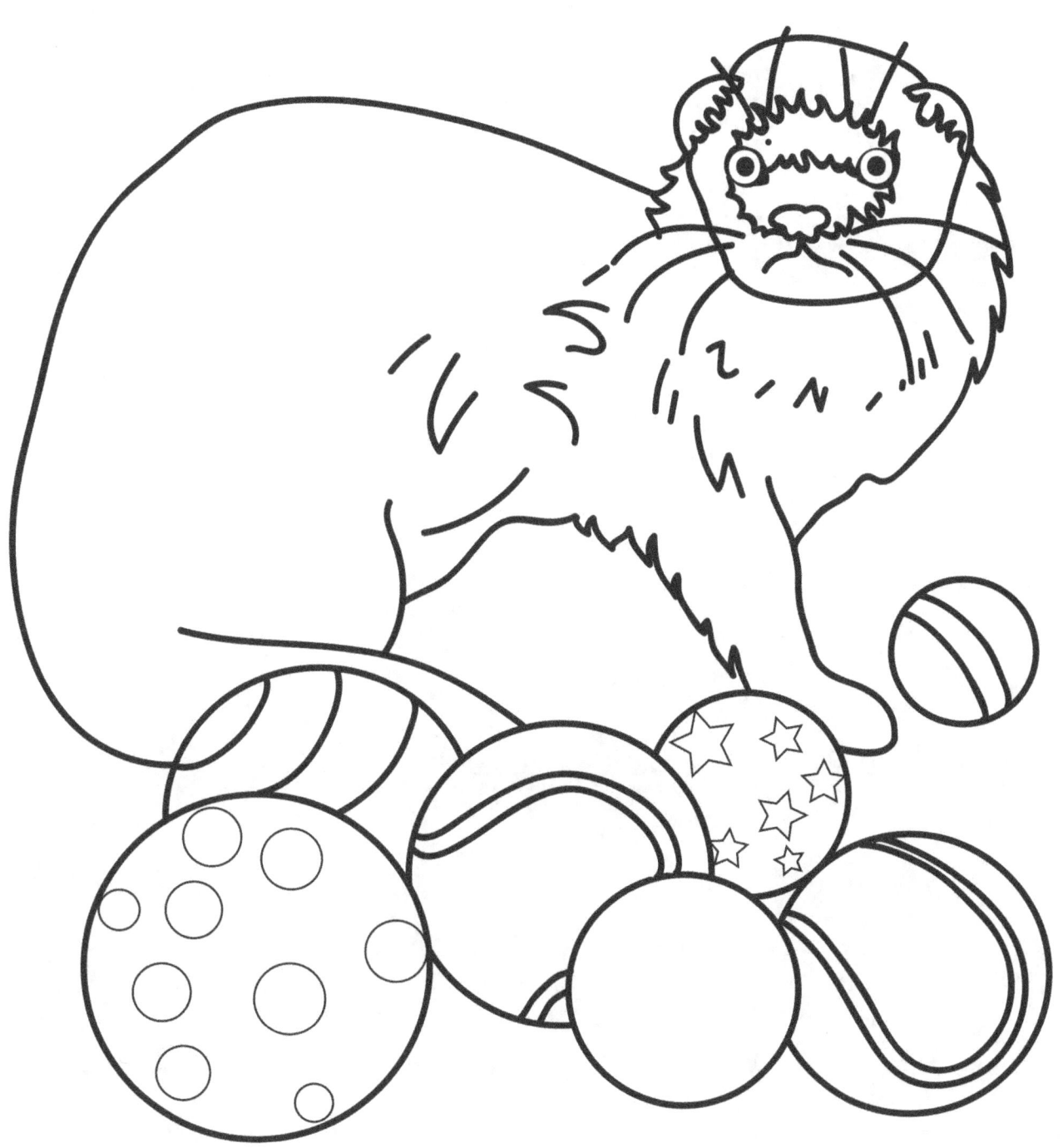

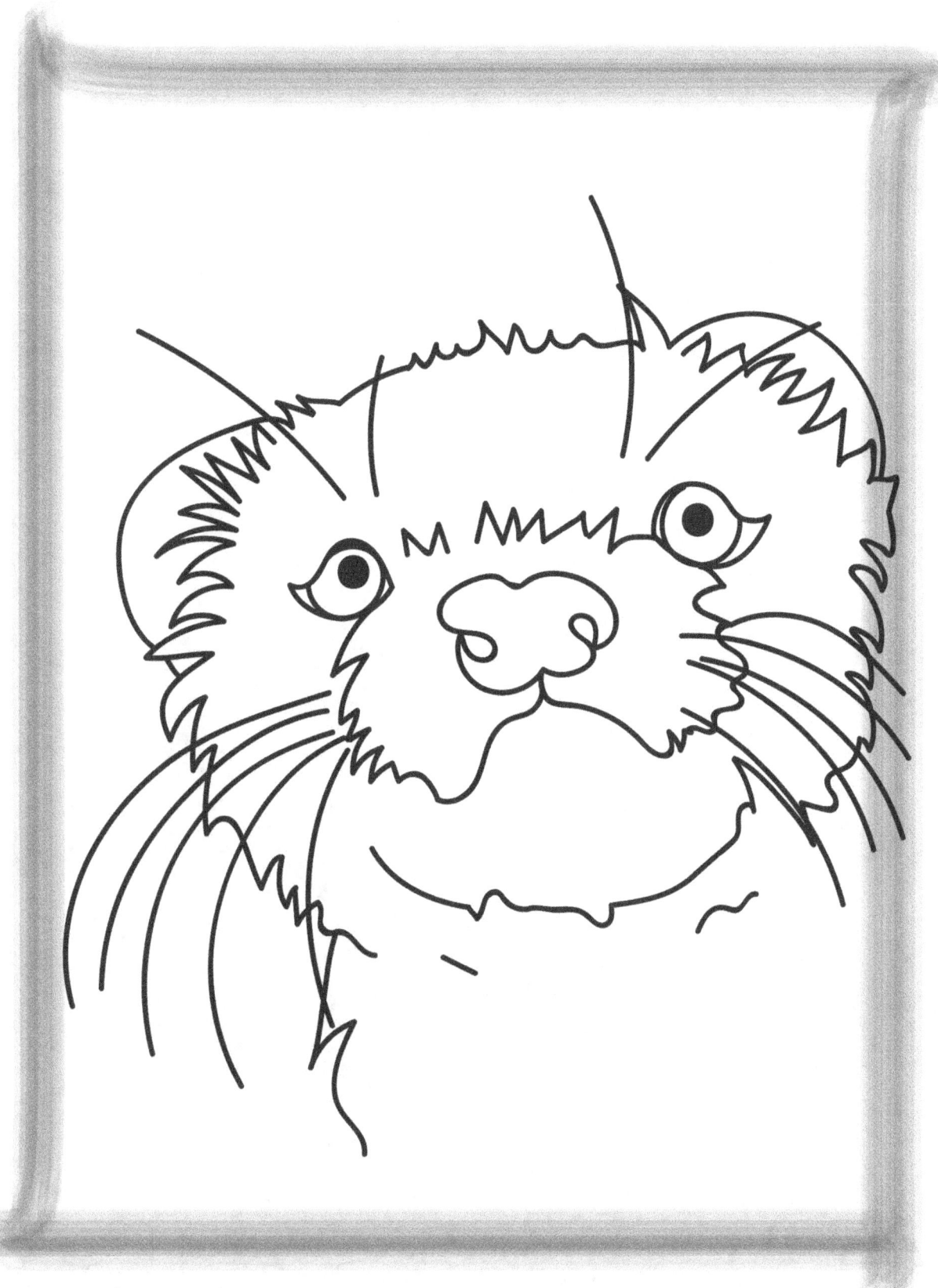

# FERRET LOVER

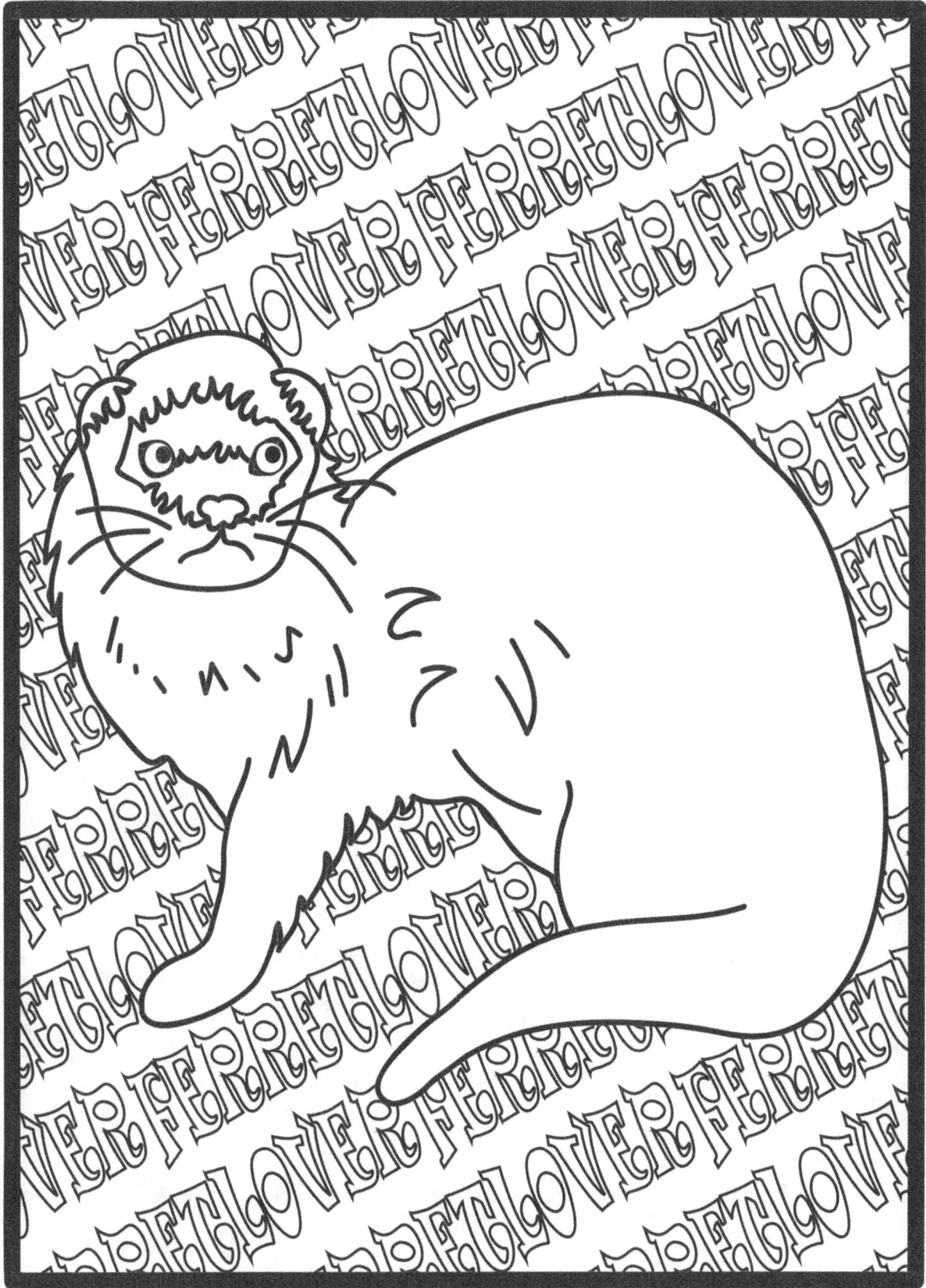

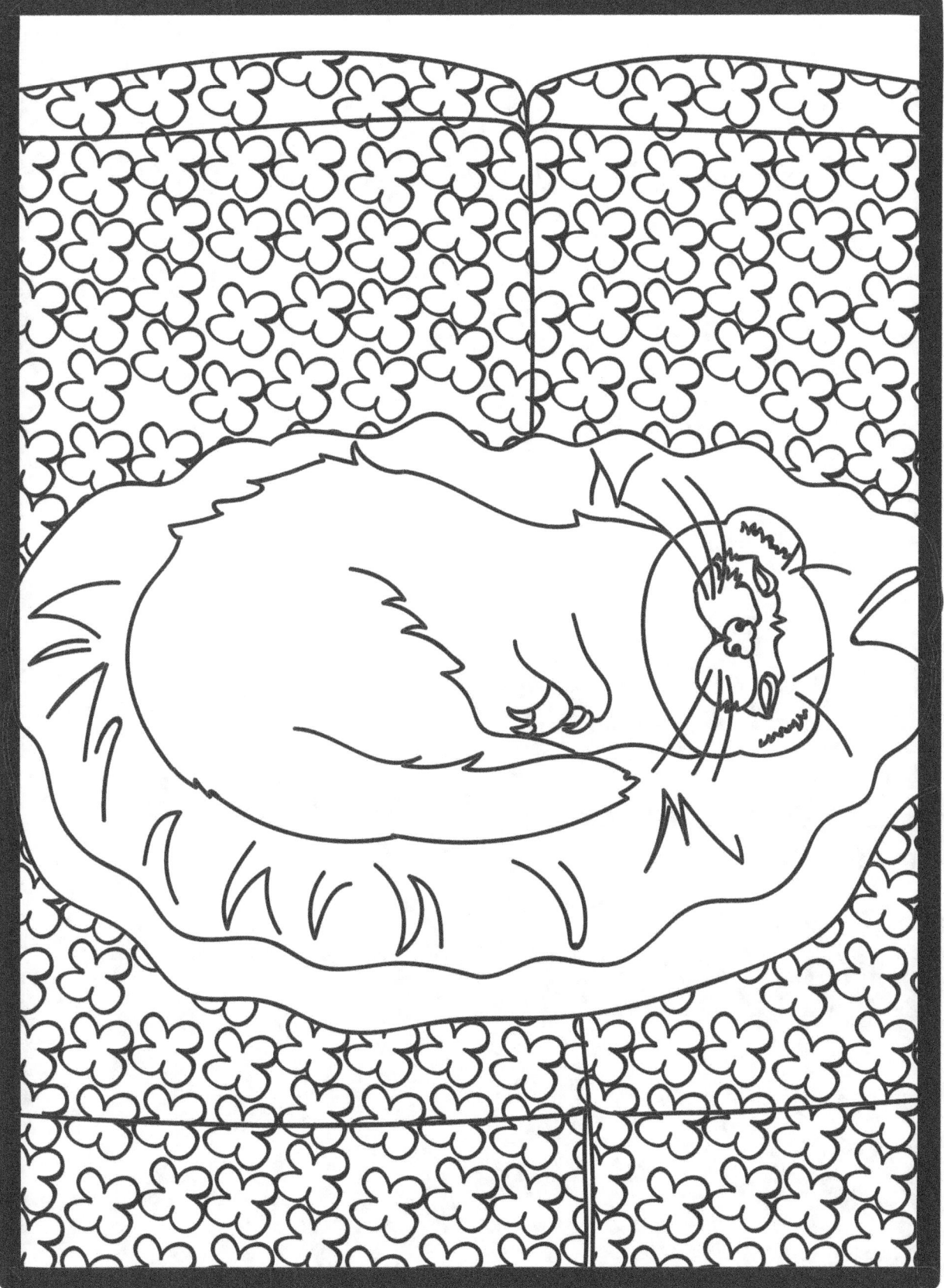

ferrets
make me happy

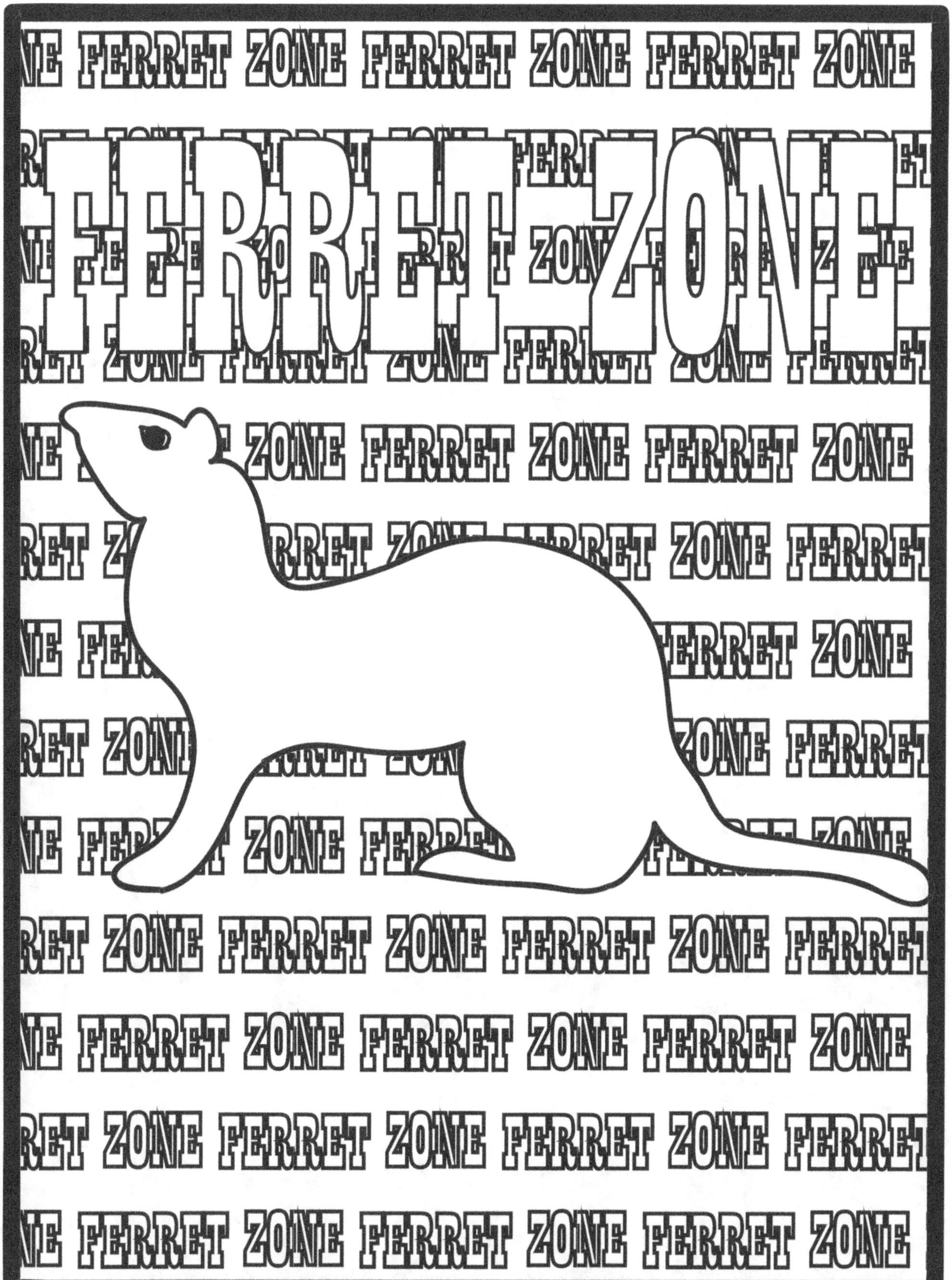
FERRET ZONE

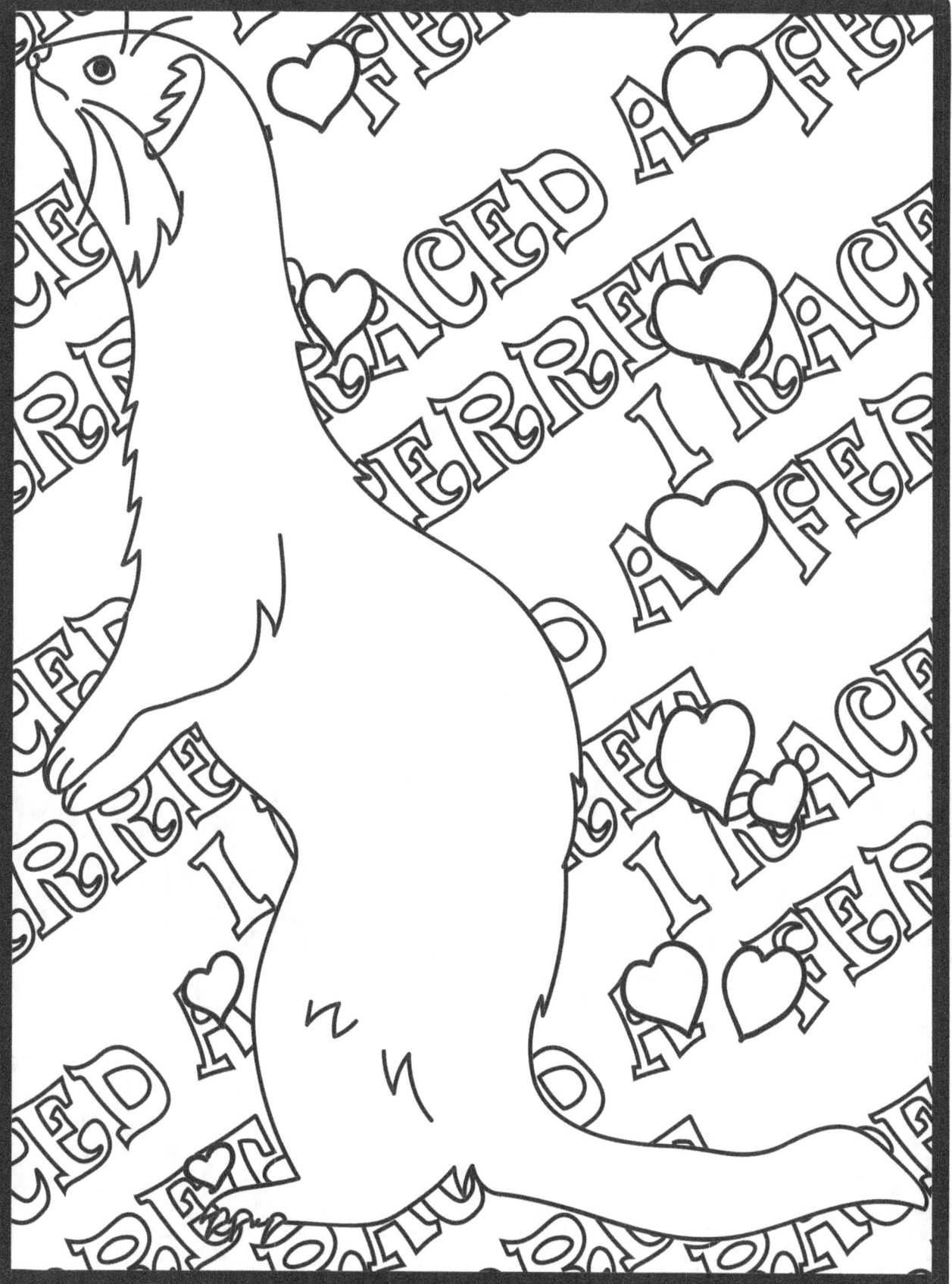

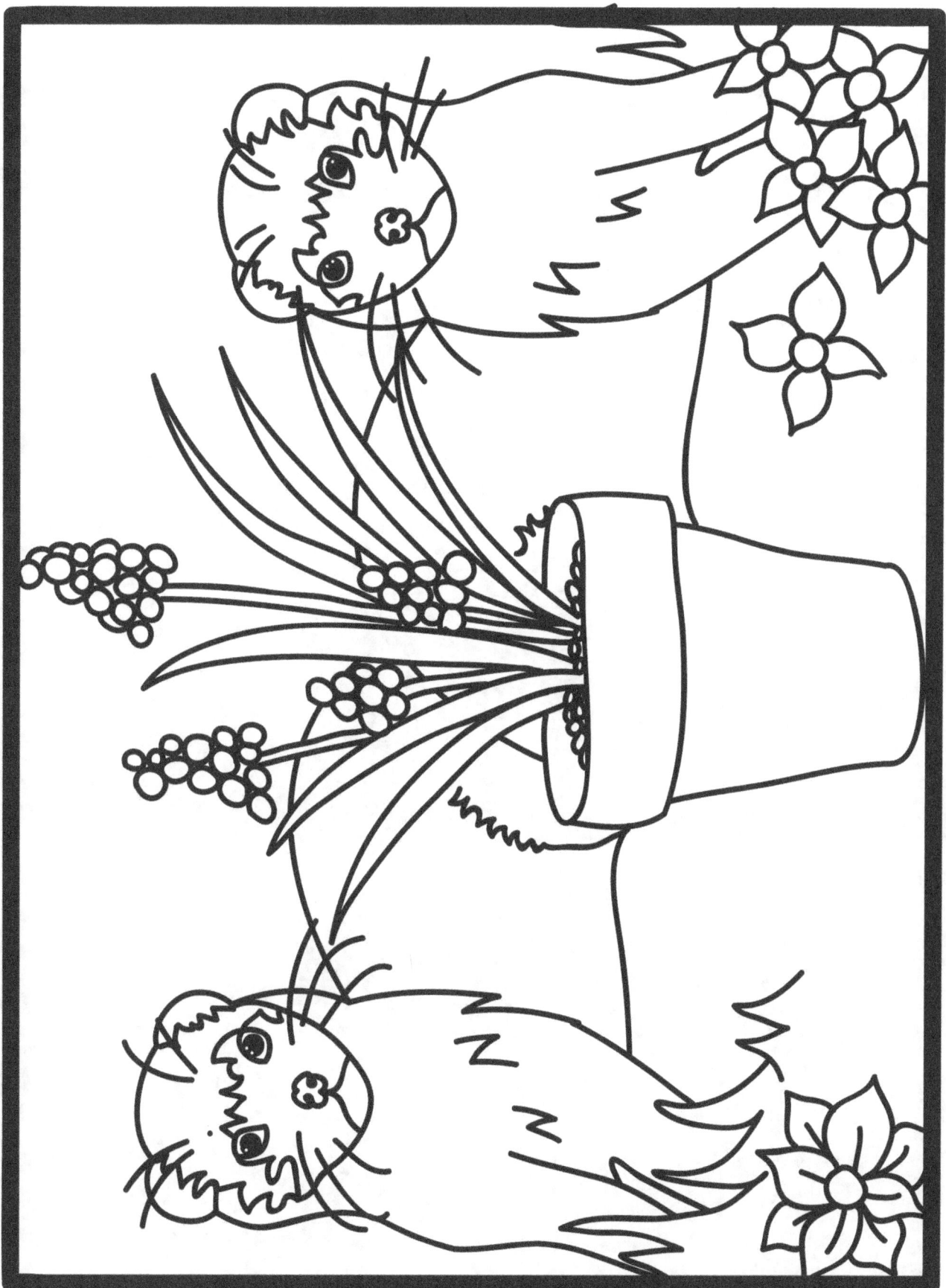

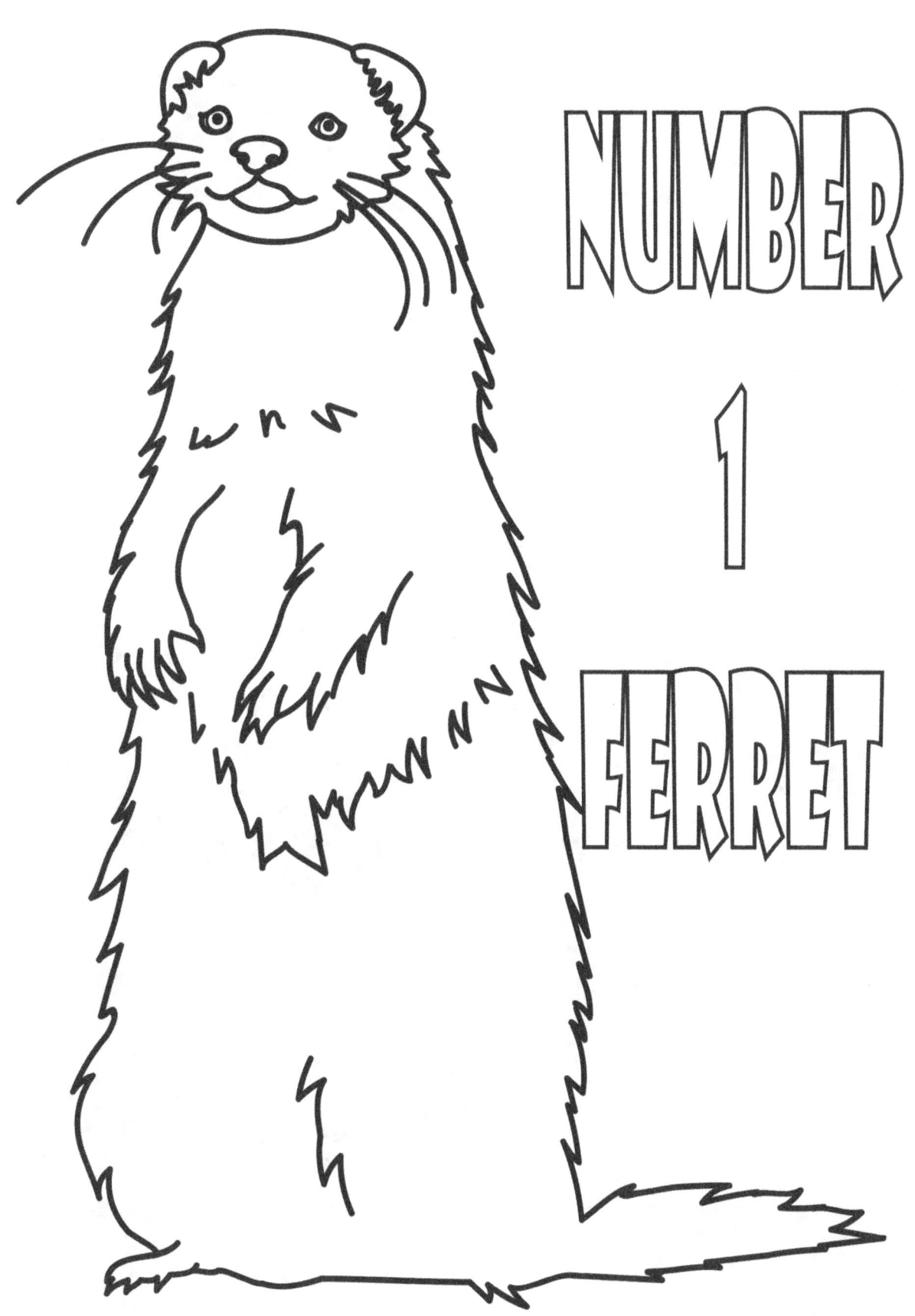

NUMBER

1

FERRET

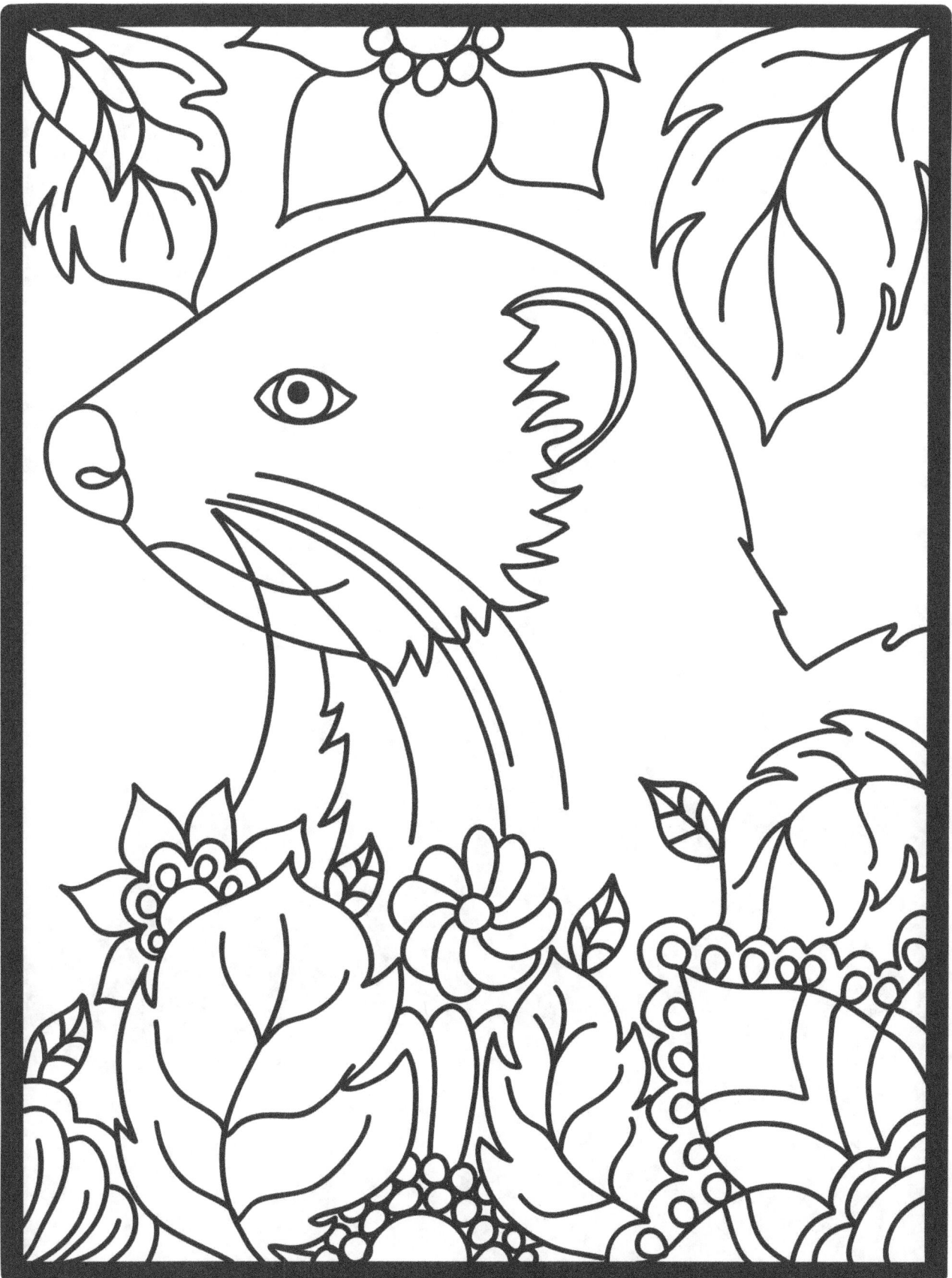

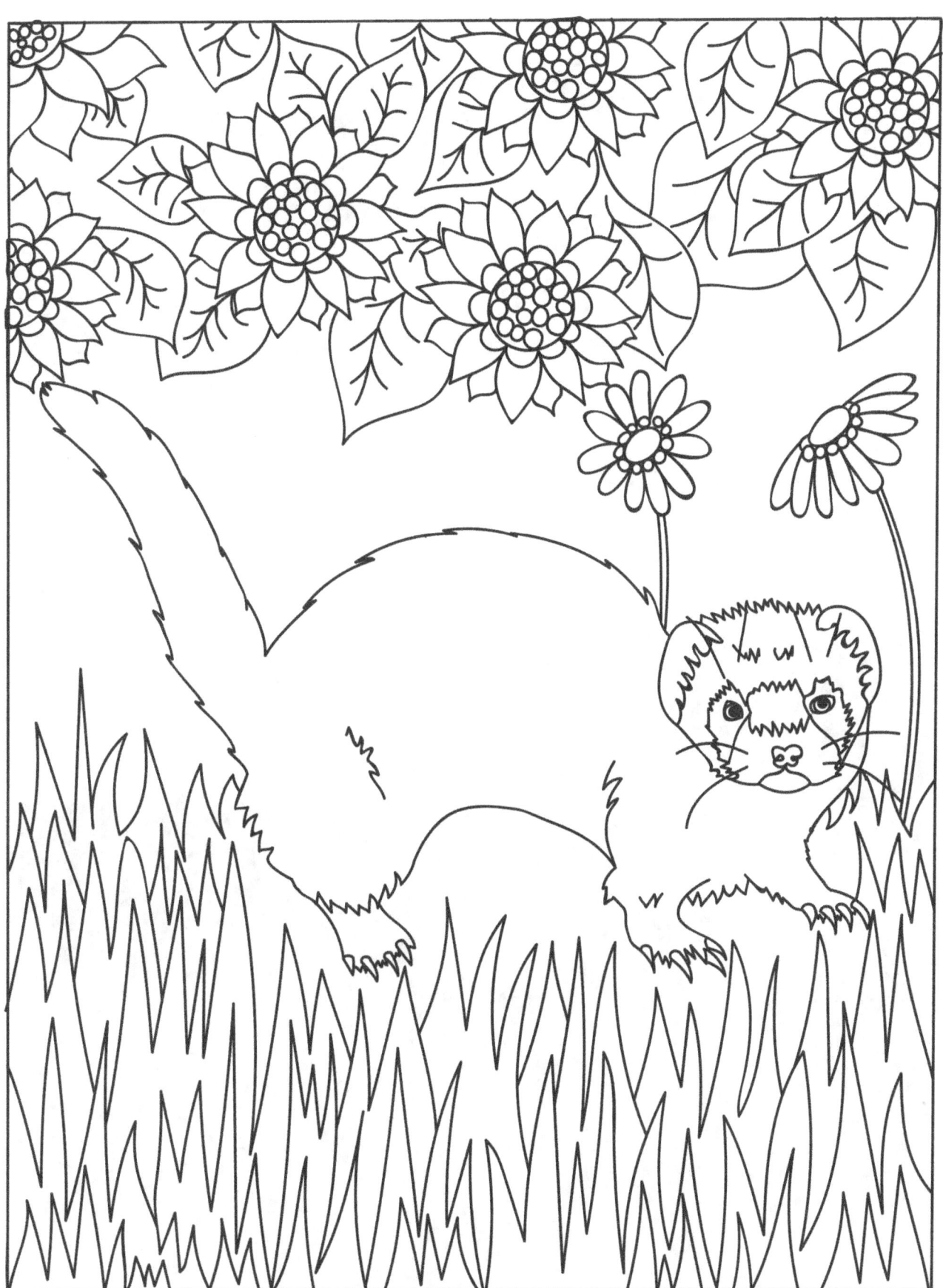

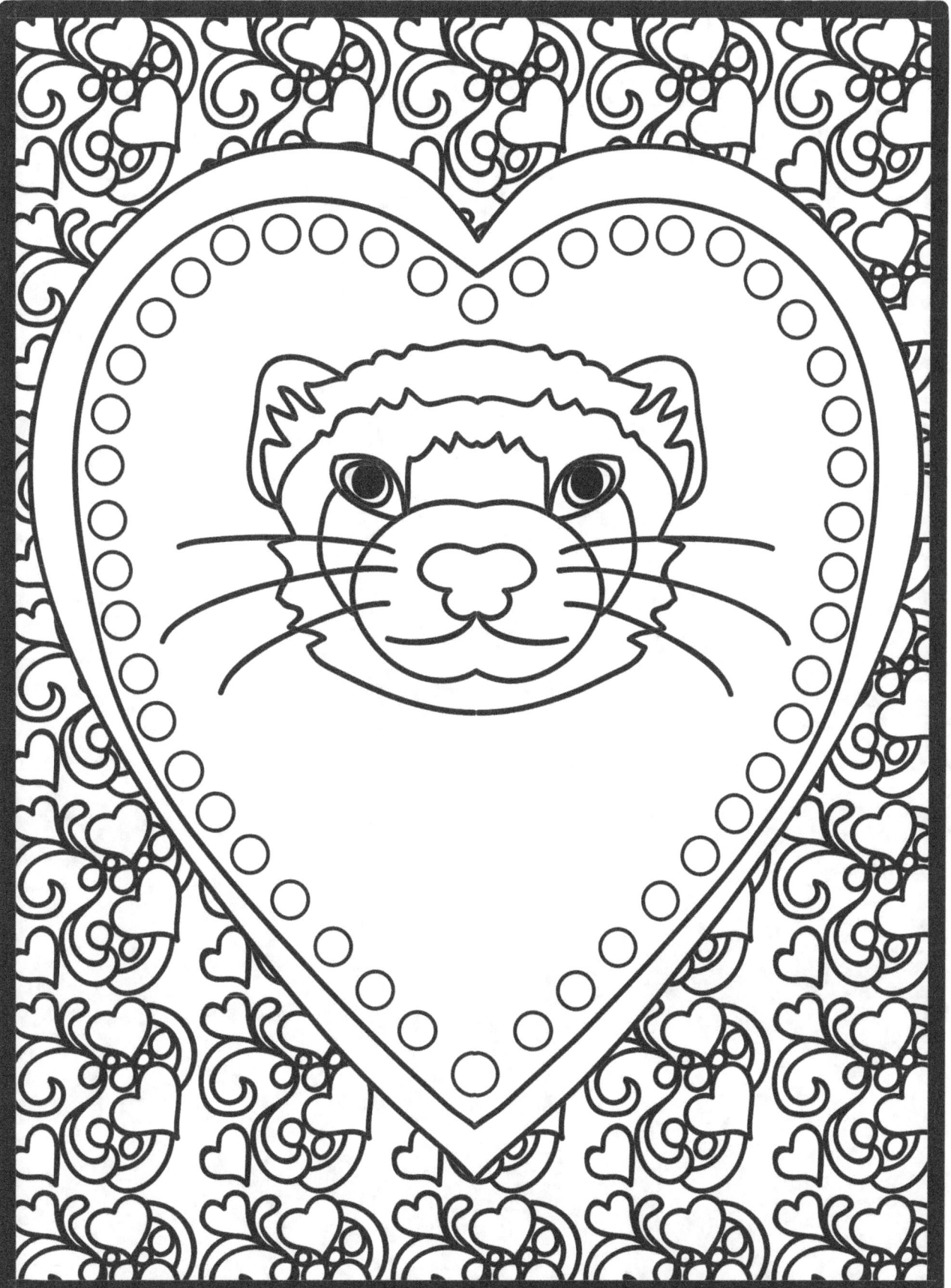

# COLOR TEST PAGE

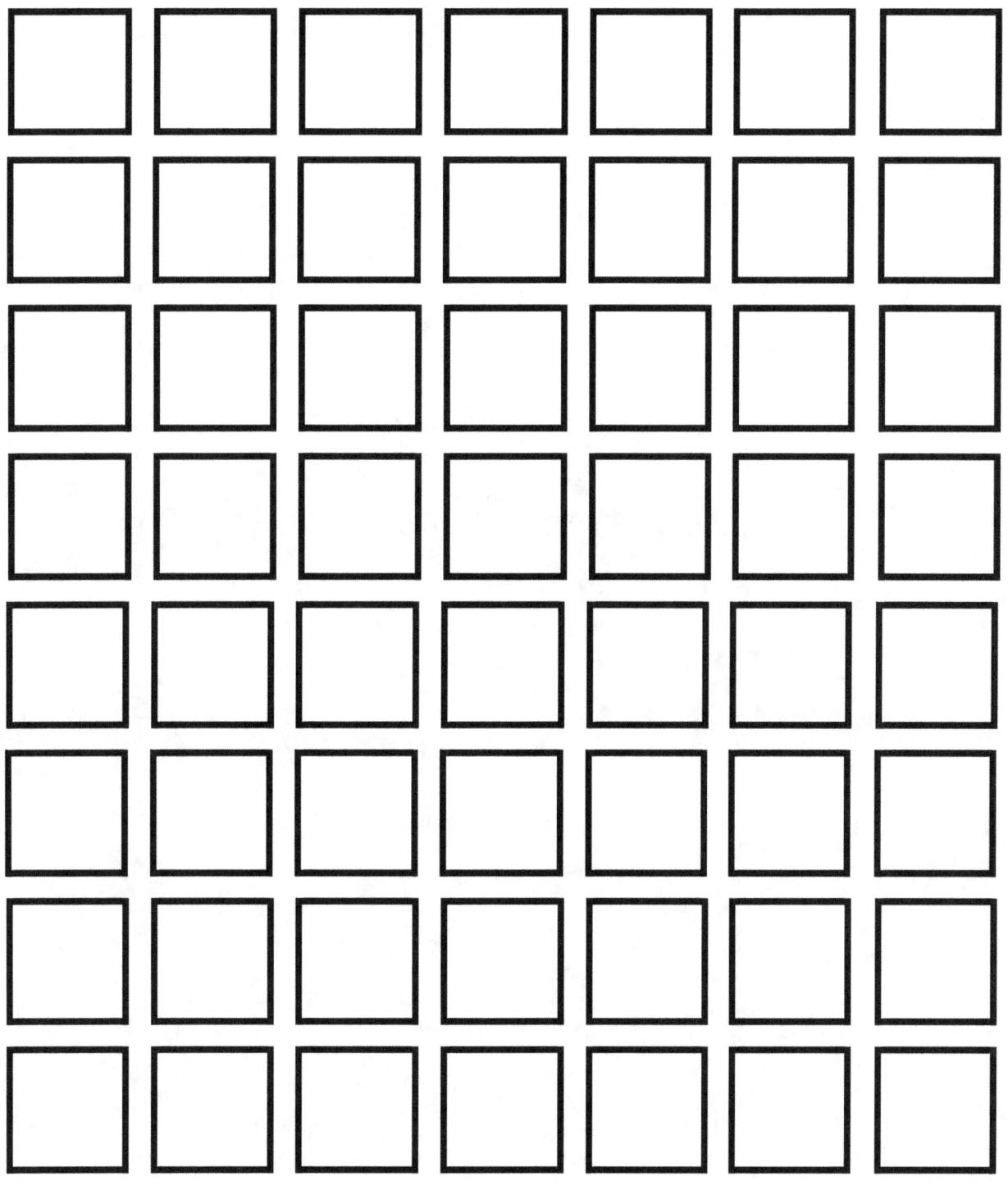

# COLOR TEST PAGE

www.ingramcontent.com/pod-product-compliance
Lightning Source LLC
Chambersburg PA
CBHW081015170526
45158CB00010B/3053